NO KISSES
FOR THE SINNER

SCOTT SHAW

BUDDHA ROSE PUBLICATIONS

No Kisses for the Sinner
Copyright © 1988 by Scott Shaw
www.scottshaw.com
All Rights Reserved

This book contains material protected under International and Federal Copyright Laws and Treaties. Any unauthorized reprint or use of this material is prohibited. No part of this book may be reproduced or transmitted in any form or by any means, electronic or mechanical, including photocopying, recording, or by any information storage and retrieval system without express written permission from the author or the publisher.

Front Cover Painting by Scott Shaw
Rear Cover Photograph of Scott Shaw
by Hae Won Shin
Copyright © All Rights Reserved

First Edition 1989
eBook Edition 2010
Second Edition 2011

ISBN 10: 1-877792-37-3
ISBN 13: 978-1-877792-37-3

Library of Congress Control Number: 2013940235

10 9 8 7 6 5 4 3 2 1
Printed in the United States of America

NO KISSES FOR THE SINNER

INTRODUCTION

It is perhaps sad that one may only see things through their own perception/though they may try and claim to do otherwise.

It is also sad that though one may believe another to have the ability to be something other than what they are: what they are is simply that, what they are.

This is the story and the case of her, and the sad truth being, what I believed she could become, was, in fact, not what she was. We both paid the price.

1

the sun bleeds
its warm presence unto me as I lay
dying
stabbed in the heart
like some drunken warrior
confounded by purpose
confused by reason
while illusion dances upon my
soul

    and the sun bleeds its
purpose unto me
    whispering it reluctance of
coming forth
    to break the spell the spell
    of a relentless night

2

and in the ending passion
of an ending night
of an ending love
ending so fast /ending so soon

oh it is so true

and the situations surround me
no where to run
desire in its purest form
wished for

      she says she wished for me

prayed for

      I have been asked for before

and it closes in
no place to run
no way out
my car is trapped
blocked by another ride
behind it
so unfair
I can not move

and she, she sings
"hey now, hey now."

and she, she asks me,
"would you like to be in a
relationship with me?"

and here I am
here I sit
go/stay?
no way to know

        and all the passion
        is lust in visions
        of what never is

        I suppose
        I wished
        I prayed
        for her as well
        but it all seems so strange
        my dreams/my desires
        so unanswered

        and yet, here they are

        answered in such a way

        but like I have long said,

"any dream will do."
well any dream it is
any dream/any reason
but...
just but...
its touch
its vision could have been
so much sweeter
its touch
so much more pure

3

ah, the midnight hour has come
it whispers of its passion
it whispers of the mystic wind
so, good night
and remember
remember everything

4

in the love
the love that loves me now
never is there a space
a space so pure
so pure it hurts

they promise you everything
      everything
      everything
      everything
           it sounds so poetic

    so poetic
    so much of nothing
    they promise you love
    so much love it will hurt

    but in reality, it hurts to
think of
    being in love with her

    but my heart pounds
    my head spins
    and I have no place left to
run
    no where at all

as my current love lies next to me
asleep

asleep in *never-never-land*
la-la-land
6:00 A.M.
she sleeps
I should go to sleep
and move onto another/a different
dream

5

I saw a picture of her
a picture sitting upon a living
room table

    slightly out of focus
    the colors faded into the
sunlight
    but her form
    was placed into infinity
    her look
    her glance
    the image of the goddess

    the image of the goddess
    but not the one
    which I have come to know

her photograph
faded by the light
faded by the focus
distant
hazy
a forgotten goddess
she has forgotten it herself
leaving her body to be used
her mind to be stolen

and when that was all completed
she handed herself to me
to me
too late
nothing could be repaired

6

I woke
to her asian eyes this morning
early morning
her time
not mine

I woke
to her asian eyes
and they were not covered
with the make-up
I had seen the night before

I woke and her face
it was not painted with the colors
I have come to expect

her eyes
they were simple
no longer
were they scared
from the years
of gaining
external wisdom
by and for external thought

      yes, they were almost free
      yes, they were almost new

I woke
to her asian eyes this morning
and they glowed the radiance
of ancient purity/ancient thought
the promise of poetry
which I had never seen in them
before

7

she asks,
"why don't you ever want to go out and be social?"

"sorry babe, I'm not a social guy."

she says,
"why don't you want to meet my friends?"

"because we have nothing in common."

"but they think I am making all this up.

they think I am making you up."

"you are."

8

force feed me a cup of illusion
yes, I do need a dream
a dream
any dream
yes, any dream will do

force feed me a cup of illusion
in the dim light
of her asian eyes

force feed me
please

force feed me a cup of salvation

or must I run away
run to where the visions are pure
run to where there is sweet
freedom
run to where there are no walls
and illusions come true

force feed me a cup of forgiveness
for yes, I have sinned
I have looked
I have seen

I have taken a hold of a dream
a dream in the dream of
where any dream will do

I have held it
I have taken it
I have known it
I did so as I saw that
it was not what I wanted
not what I needed
not what I thought it would be
        at all

I took it
I held it
I knew its forms was imperfect
yet, I took it anyway

force feed me a cup of salvation
for yes, I have sinned
I believed any dream will do
well, any dream is what I got
and it was unworthy
still the same

9

her blood drips upon me
she softly rubs it in

spread your love disease upon me
spread it
make sure that there can be no
escape

once it seemed to matter
now it all appears too late
     loss and gain
     all the same
     I can never escape

she raises her body
her blood drips upon me
she moves slowly
applying it softly

spread your love disease
leave me
no escape

10

I woke up in the morning
my morning
12:00 P.M., or so
I made my way into the bathroom
for the traditional
shower and shave

as I stand there
thinking of the night before
of the woman
who had been in my arms
as I stand there thinking
of a million reasons
to leave her alone
a million ways
to get her to do the same
I look down
and there upon my shoulder
intertwined with my long blond
hair
was a long straight black hair
one of hers
from the night before

she gets up 7:30 A.M.
work, she has to be to

I am left alone
to the mystical breakfast
on the shore
and the memories
of the night(s) before

but there is so much more to life
so much more to love
than reasons
beyond no good reason
and lasting embraces
in the night

11

can it be
that the forgiveness
lies in the arms of a stranger
a stranger who is known by many

> can it be known
> can it be held
> can I find
> can I feel it anywhere at all

I thought that it may be found
in her arms/in her kiss

> her kiss
> I have known it
> as many other before
> she can not remember the number
> lost count
> in lost time
> and more than one is one too many for me

> but me too
> long ago I lost count
> so who am I to judge

once the secret it is lost
once the secret is known
and than there is nothing
    left to prove

with nothing left to know
nothing left to prove
knowledge loses all its meaning

teach me what I have never known

12

she lives
just above the sunset strip
just up the street from
    the whiskey a-go-go

a dream of the clothed in leather
a dream for those who
worship the illusions of the night

I lived it
that dream
but that dream was so long ago

    lived it/had it
    it gave me no reason

but there she sits
her apartment on the hill
believing that her location
makes her who she is
makes her more
something
less than nothing

but when you live
in the noise

the crowds
next to the polluted want-a-bes
all you embrace is their pollution

not the true wisdom
of the night

13

the love of illusion
yes, the love of delusion
and how it comes down so hard
so hard on me
so hard on what is
and what is longed for
or better said, what isn't

isn't, isn't

and it has been had
so many times before
before, where all the dead dreams
lie

tomorrow, where all the fantasies
live

live in their immaterialness
live, but are not real
yet, they live just the same

14

life in the mainstream
alive but so unreal
real is here
but it feels so unreal
so much less
than it could have been

you are breathing
your mainstream onto me
you make me feel false
unreal/untrue

but here is where we are
and this is what we have to deal
with

what is this?
what it is,
isn't it?

in all its perfection

15

the kiss
it is oh so alluring
the lie
so allusive
but let us lay down here
lay down
and hold one another
and pretend
that before never existed

16

confusion
this dance goes on and on
will it ever stop/can it ever stop

choose love
as it stares at me
the past
will it ever be gone /can it ever be gone

gone today
gone tomorrow
gone forever
forever and ever

if it is gone than why does it haunt me so

kiss me
one more time
convince me
to stay with you another day
convince me
try to make me believe

convince me
I want to believe
convince me
of my confusion

17

she telephones me
she says,
"yes, I will quit my job.
        and you will do
        something flaky.
    like leave me again.
    I know it, I just know it."

"your instincts
    they serve you well,"
        I answer.

"But make a choice
    a chance
    for a dream
        as momentary as that
        dream may be
    a chance
    to live
    to feel
    to do nothing
    to accomplish nothing
    the essence of life
    so make a choice."

18

now it is not
that she is not a serious babe
and it is not
that she doesn't know how to
dress
it is just
that she never wants
to take walks by the ocean
feel the wind blow
in the mountain air
it is just that she prefers
new york city
over san francisco
and she just does not know how
to do nothing
nothing at all

now it is not
that I do not love her
as far as love may go
and it is not
that I would not want to hold her
forever
it is just that she does not know
how to dream

to dream
the answer of the ancients
the key to the mysteries
    the love of the love for
    the love
like the wind
you never see it
    but you can feel that it
    is there

19

I almost wish
that I could marry her
I almost wish
that I loved her more
I almost wish
I had never lied to her
I almost wish
a lot of things

but things
they never seem to end
and the world
well, it goes on and on

>   the world goes on
>   time ticks on
>   life moves on
>   and love
>   well, it fades

but in all the realms
of *never-never-land*
the land that surrounds all time
all is
what ever it is
and what never was

will always be
I can not erase it
though I have tried

    love lost
    love that kills
    point the gun at me
    and fire at will

20

I look to my side
there lays a black hair
a black hair
from the woman
the woman I made love to this
evening

and though I can never love her
again
I will let the black hair rest

rest in its place
I will let it
sleep next to me tonight

> one more night
> for the memories
> one more night
> for the dreams
> one more night
> for no reason at all
> one more night
> for the screams

21

she asked me
are we the same as you two were
am I the same as she
did our needs bring us together
like your needs led you to her

no, it is not need
that brought us together
desire is a far better word
desire and need
are so far apart
like desire has made me
walk away from you

now, I am not saying
we were not in love
and I am not saying
it did not feel good
but desire
no, it is not need
and desire
it always seems to die
when the illusion wears off

22

and the kisses
embrace the day
the touch
embraces the night
and when all are interweaved
all are intertwined
the truth
it be spoken
the truth
be spoken to the few

and therefore
and thereof
the lies
they no longer matter
the actions
they no longer care
and the love
it is spread
deeply in the night
lasting until the day

than the day
speaks its goodbyes

23

the kisses are for those
who eat the late night pies
the dreams are for those
that live
the love is for those
who are believers
and tonight
is for those of us
who never look back

    is there ever a kiss
        misplaced
    a love longed for
    more than lust
    a feeling embraced
    than turned away
    a night
    that just goes on too long

    every dream has its price
    for life is filled with lies

    every love
    has a destiny to end
    life is simply too short
        a time

and when there is no more use
in pretending
and when there is
no more reasons why

a kiss becomes just a kiss
a dream just a dream
and then
mysticism fills the air

24

the kiss
it looks so sweet
but it feels so deadly
attraction/distraction
I've lived on the outskirts of hell

gray, it is not so clean
not so shiny
or is it simply dirty white

gray is the color of the city
I have slept on the outskirts of
hell

there is no place to run to
no place left to hide
it all is the same
one moment flowing to the next
one feeling into the other
the next to the other
I have been embraced by the
outskirts of hell

25

her words,
they speak to me,
she says,
    "well, at least I have lived.
       you know,
        I could write a book.
    a book, just like you write.
    what would you have rather
I had been,
    a nice little girl
     growing up like those
around me?"

    "maybe, yes maybe."

living it is for fools
fools who believe the lie
the lie
of supply and demand
conquest and conquer
fools, who never will see
that all the living
adds up to nothing

    maybe we should sit
    and watch

maybe it would be better
that way
simply let the world go by
in its time
and believe
that gain and experience
mean nothing at all

maybe
I do not know

for there are mystics
who danced upon the path
who walk on both sides
of the wall
mystics like me who live
mystics like me who dream

believing that every
      take down
is a lift up
every lie
is eventual truth

so maybe
I do not know

but both sides of the wall
it is a difficult way
difficult and distant
in all the realms of mind
back and forth
going nowhere
going everywhere
where, is no place at all

so maybe
just maybe
it is truth
not to give in
truth
to run away
truth
to sit and watch
as the water settles to mud
and the truth
to merges with I do not care

it is not easy
that I know
for the world
hands its hooks
into everyone

easy or hard
one leads to the other

the different to the same

day to night
night to day

    maybe, yes maybe

26

I almost believed
that we were meant to be
yes, I almost believed
that we could be
could be forever

        forever and ever and ever
        yes, I almost believed
        that we were butter
        melting into each other

yes
and when I look into your eyes
when I don't look too deep
and when I try not to see

        see who you were
        see what you were
        yes, I almost believe
        that I could love you forever
        forever and ever and ever

and when the wheel spins around
and the truth comes down
it is like a knife
in my heart

tearing me apart
because I almost believed
that you and I
could have been forever
forever and ever and ever

so I try to tell myself
do not open your eyes
keep them closed
and just compromise
never look too far
never look to deep
but the truth comes down
and the messages they speak
but I almost believed
that it was a dream
yes, I almost believed
that you were forever
forever and ever and ever

27

I called her
on the telephone
spoke to her
on the telephone line
it meant nothing
not anything at all

    zero in a zero world

    now I could go
    to her place tonight
    for you know that
    I do have the keys
    I could go there
    for I know that
    she waits for me
    I could go there
    and make nothing
    equal even less

    do you love me
    she asks

    I hang up

now the games and dance go on
and on
and I've got no more time

    no more time
    for my lies
    to mean nothing

    but than nothing
    does not mean
    anything at all

I always initiate the first blow
strike hard
is the rule of the game
never let your opponent move first
always keep the advantage clear

if the opponent connects
if their blow hits home
strike back hard
devastate them
take no prisoners
none at all

love and lust
and relationships

they are all for the fool
play them
play them well
I do

I called her on the telephone line
there is no reason why
I call the game
call it to win it
one more time
I push the drama
push it to one more scene

> everything is
> as everything isn't
> and there is no reason why
> good night/goodbye
> she wants me
> she wants the game
> she wants the lies
> that I have told her
> she wants the fantasy

but love is love
only by definition

definitions
they always seem to change

let them change
as change will change
like the wind
in the california winter sky

the last words that I spoke to her
a hang up
to her question

    it said, yes
    yes, I do
    let me come to you
    please heal all of my pain

but nothing ever equals anything
zero is still the same
the same
it never seems to stay that way
    the same
a hang up on the telephone line

28

did I tell you
that I lied
when I told
that I loved you

>no reason
>is the best reason
>of all

I lied
when I told you
that I loved you
I lied to you
I lied to myself

you had what it took to get me
you did not have what it took to
keep me
keep me with you

>and the passion of existence
>and the prospect of forever
>it never has the ability
>to last
>so when the kisses come in
>and the dreams die young

the flowers that may bloom
        tomorrow
have all that it takes
to give birth to a new dream

29

she cried to me on the telephone
a pay phone on melrose
she cried
for my love
cried, like I have cried for love

       for love
       love that she wants
       she cried
       for me to be with her
       I wish I could
       she cried
       I will cry
       but I can not allow myself to
       not now
       not until I am alone
       when my tears
       will not be heard
       by her,
        my west hollywood
       chinese princess
       at a pay phone on melrose
       alone...

30

a collect call
comes on the telephone lines
why is it
that the babe's always call me
collect

      a collect call comes in
          a collect call goes on

"do you want me to come over?"
"why," I ask
"because you love me."
"I do?"

but then the subject changes
    she tells me
    that she would be
        slapping me
    if I were standing next to her

"a lot of *cha-cha's* going by," she
says
"what's a *cha-cha?*" I ask
"you know,
    the kind of girl you always
fall in love with.

that kind of girl that you
always want to leave.
you know, *cha-cha's,*
party girls,
chinese party, girls,
like I used to be."

I guess she knows me well
and I guess it is true
that if I had been there
she would have slapped me
for checking out the scene

but isn't what you once were
the foundation
the formation
of what you are

she and I
her mind
my lies
it never did add up to two
so with her dollars in tow
her mind on me
with her finger
on the push buttons

I get a collect telephone call.

"do you want me to come over?"
"why?"

31

I wish all the hours of time
spent talking to her
on the telephone line
could equal its weight in creativity
equal its weight in gold

the words that are spoken
tears and fears
love and lies
dreaming
as we both tend to do

I wish when all was said
and when all was done
it could mean more
than simple foolish emotions
simple foolish sounds

than all would be
of so much more validity

creativity
turned to gold

32

she sends me flowers
she sends them to my door
she sends me roses
roses by the dozen

with each arrival
there comes a card

I love you

I love you forever

forever
forever

today they arrived
the flowers, in the evening
the flowers, of the evening
they came with a card
a card that said

still dreaming...

well, dream on my asian
sweetheart
dream

all that you can dream
dream
forever and ever
dream
that you will be with me again

for maybe if you dream
dream just hard enough
maybe if you dream
dream with enough intensity
maybe if you dream
forever and ever
than you may see me again

for whenever the vision has faded
whenever the truth comes out
and whenever there is just too
much known
and not enough felt
there is one reason left
a reason to walk away

so send me flowers
if you have the inclination
I will receive them in style
send me roses

if you have the money
but you did not lay them at my
feet

      so kiss tomorrow
      as it embraces you
      kiss it
      as you have kissed me
      kiss it hello
      as I kiss you goodbye

      goodbye
      forever and ever

33

I could not help but fell the
distance
the distance
as I glanced into your eyes

as love dances
as love always seems to do
it has separated
separated her and I

reached the point of flux
where her world
can not meet mine
mine can not see hers

so the movement
it is in motion
the lessening of the love
it has begun

she will chase
I will run
but in the end
it will be the same
it will be gone

34

her body
it has lost all of its illusion
no longer
do I long
to embrace within her arms
intimacy has not replaced the
boredom
love has never grown
in the place that infatuation once
held

there seems only one answer
the answer
it can only remain the same

as in all those in front of me
and all those before
the answer is to walk away

now I wish it could have been
more silent
silent parting
the ultimate art
but it grew loud
made itself notices

loud
it made itself heard

with all that is lost
and with all that is gained
and all that is once loved
than no longer loved
there seems to be a rhythm
seems to be a familiarity
seems to be a sign
they all seem so much alike
but it describes only
the same pain

her body
it has lost all of its illusion
no longer
do I long
to embrace within its arms
intimacy has not replaced the
boredom
love has never grown
in the place that infatuation once
held

35

some women you can not love
some women you do not want to
love
some women you pretend to love
some women you almost love
and some women
the more you love them
the more it hurts
so all you can do is run away

me, I run very well

36

a rose pedal
lays on the floor
on the floor
under a chair
a neo-modern
nuevo-high tech chair
a chair
I purchased at a thrift store
$10.00

the rose pedal lay there
from a dozen roses
given to me by a girl
a girl which I tried to love
I tried hard

oh, she was so beautiful
dressed in her west hollywood
glam-slam style

> eyes, they were so asian
> lips, they were painted
>   so red
> hair, it was so black
> love, it could have been

yes, it is true
for I was fooled by a pretty face

a pretty face
like the roses

the roses they were red
yet they faded
they died
they fell apart
one of the pedals
now lay upon my floor

    red
    dark red
    like her painted lips

her lips
they would caress me
they would paint my body
leave their imprint
upon my soul

    lips
    red
    imprint

like it has left on my life

the rose pedal
lay on my floor
under my neo-modern
nuevo-high tech chair
from the thrift store

the pedal red
it reminds me
of the roses
which she gave me

the pedal
it reminds me
of a woman
which I tried to love
I tried very hard
it is true

I was fooled
by a beautiful face

the rose pedal
it is no longer alive
dead like our love

the little of it that there was

gone
faded
fading like the memory
of a west hollywood
glam-slam chinese girl
who seduced me
tried to make me love her
promised me everything
but it did not work

it all lay in its decomposingness

our love
the memory
just like
the rose pedal
which lay upon my floor

37

she cries on the telephone
I have heard her tears before
she cries
I ask her
to please calm down
but I hear the tears ringing
as they stab
a tender spot in my soul

she cries on the telephone
I have heard these tears before
I tell her
I will come over
try to make her feel better
she wants to know why
for I can not promise her
tomorrow

all my words of forever
turned into being nothing but lies
she is right
I am wrong
I have failed
by not being able
to love her fully
not being able to

but promising her that I could

she cries on the telephone
I have heard these tears before
I have made her cry too many
times

38

what do you do
when your dream dies
or a least the closest thing to it
so far/thus far

blood red lips
asian eyes
a girl
from glam-slam
west hollywood

I have painted her
a thousand times

what do you do
when what was
is washed away
wiped clean
by your own hands
put to rest
by your own deeds

is it
what was there
or was it
what was lacking

that made me continue
to stay
continue to run away

was it
or is it
they forever
leave a blank answer
in my mind

and yes, I remember the dream
and yes, I remember the dare
and yes, I remember desire
to find someone just like her

and yes, I know the longing
and yes, I the pain

the desire to have
to hold
and then let go
only to desire again

so closes another chapter
of my life

no longer can it be said
that it is still an open book
with pages remaining to be read

what do you do
when you run so hard from
someone
and when you stop
and look around
and find yourself
all alone

and what do you do
when the near perfect dream dies

39

she tells me
that she forgets
forgets what it is like to
    sleep with me
I tell her
remember
remember forever and ever
for that is all that you now have
now
    the memories

and love gets old
and she gets angry
angry
that I do not
fall at her hallowed feet

and love dies
where it was never born
gone
forever more

40

and when my eyes are closed
it is magic/pure magic

the magic it has increased with time

and when we are together
together and in each other's arms
if I don't think too hard
I never want to be in another's

love it is not for strangers
love it is only for the fool
love, if only it were the only thing
but all the world goes on and on

and when you cry
     I cry
when you feel lost
     I am lost
and when you have those feeling
of not wanting to go on
they are no different
than the ones I have come to know

but my eyes, it seems
they can not stay closed

my dreams
through the years
have become quite defined
and if love were enough
to heal all the wounds
than the love which you have
      given me
would cure all my pain

you have touched me
like no one before
that is why I write this verse
you have given me gifts
which no one in the past
ever took the time to give
that is why I wish
it was all so different

and if it were only the love
than the only love
you would be
but haunting obsessing memories
they continue to follow us
close on our trail
from a world of yours
of which I want no part

kiss me my love
the girl I wished for
and I will kiss you
a kiss from the man
you dreamed of
      a kiss it will be
      a kiss forever more
      a kiss goodbye

yes, I have grown to love
love as much
as most before
but a kiss
it will be
a kiss goodbye
for my eyes can not remain closed

and the magic
though it is strong
does not have the strength
to make them stay that way

but when my eyes are not open
it is such magic
magic as I have never known
before

it is the magic
that I will remember
remember as I think of you
remember
that when my eyes were closed
I loved you
like no one before

41

hours of time/telephone lines
her words they say nothing to me
hours of time/talking with no mind
the words of a fool

lie
though she doesn't know she lies
but the words they equal un-truths
just the same/all in the game
the dance
that goes on and on

promise me love
she says to me
promise me time
her words cry
promise me forever
forever and ever
promise me until death do us part

promise me

words they go so far
so far into *never-never-land*

words they equal zero

zero
the figure that describes
life and its emptiness

the hours they tick by
time misspent
time I can never get it back

but her screams to the night
the wail of her tears
the promises that she makes
and the lies
and her fears

never, never, never

so let me write these words
to compensate for her tears
let me write these words
to make something
of all the time that has been spent
all the time that has been lost

written words
her promises
and the telephone line

hours of time/telephone lines
her words they say nothing to me

hours of time/telephone lines
talking with no mind
the words of a fool

42

I suppose that I am sorry
that I have made you cry
I suppose that I am sorry
that I have brought tears
    to your eyes
I suppose
that is the case
but the truth being told
and the lies being known
it is
what has happened

and if I had been wise
if I had not been such a fool
if I had the strength
to walk away clean
than perhaps your tears
may never had needed to fall

but I was a dreamer
a dreamer
in search of a dream
    a dreamer

speaking
    what a dreamer does

    saying
            that any dream will do

well, you were that
that, anyway
a dream
that lived on
to be my nightmare
a dream
from which I had to run

but when there is no way out
there is certainly no way in
and never
sounds so much better
than forever
so the kiss goodbye
it felt so sweet
yet, it had to be dealt
in a bitter broth

so tomorrow show signs
of a new a different dream
today's sound
rings in my ears
with the tears you have cried
with the lies we have lied
and never
sounds so much better

than forever
and no longer will any dream do

I suppose that I am sorry
that I have made you cry
I suppose that I am sorry
that I have brought tears
to your eyes

43

she tells me on the telephone,
"the last thing I will ever have
from you
       is a note that says,
            fuck you."

I told her,
"I will send you some poetry."
those were the final words that I
spoke to her
I hung up

       well here it is
       and here they are

       poetry
       words

       to a woman...
       who was not
            too much of anything
       except a waste of my time
       and a reason to write

and the dreams
they call us out

the desires
they make us fall
and the screams
they go on forever
forever and ever and ever

and she could never be
what I wanted her to be
never could the past be erased
and I could never agree to be
all that she wanted of me

I could not be
the dream which she called for

so I left a note
fuck you
and I walked away

a night/a day
they all moved together
it was only a moment ago

now time goes on
as it tends to do

dreams fade/desires change
and clarity becomes all the same

    and when the moment
    where any dream will do
    fades slowly
    into the place
    where only a specific
    desire will be true
    than life ticks on
    I move on
    and the only truth
    is the closing words
    I wrote to her
    fuck you

44

yes, that is her
the one with the bright
    red lip stick
and the sunglasses on
yes, she was mine
yes, she could have been mine
forever
but it was I
who walked away

yes, that is her
the one with the jet black hair
the black leather jacket
and the chinese eyes hidden
yes, she was mine

mine for a moment
a moment in time

yes, she flowed away
flowed away
to the halls of the illusion
where all the tainted goddesses
dwell
yes, she flowed
and I have never seen her again

45

is it I
who buys the ticket
to be alone
is it I?

is it I
who makes other's choices
makes other's minds
is it I?

is it I
who can't erase
what has long ago happened
can I pretend
that it never did exist
is it I?

is it I
who is lost in the masses
lost in the form
formless as it may be
is it I?

is it I
who spins in the whirlpool
spins in the hurricane

and can not find a way out
is it I?

is it I
who longs to dream
longs to love
longs to long
is it I?

is it I
who chooses to be alone
is it I?

no, I don't think so
no

About the Author

Scott Shaw is a prolific author, actor, filmmaker, and composer. Shaw's poetry and literary fiction were first published by literary journals in the late 1970s. He continued forward to have several works of poetry and literary fiction published, in book form, during the 1980s. By the mid 1980s, after having spent years traveling extensively throughout Asia, documenting obscure aspects of Asian culture in words and on film, his writings on social science began to be published, as well. As the 1990s dawned, Shaw writings, based upon a lifelong involvement with the martial arts and eastern mysticism, began to be embraced. From this, he has authored literally hundreds of articles and a number of books on meditation, the martial arts, yoga, and Zen Buddhism; published by large publishing houses.

Books by Scott Shaw include:

About Peace:
  A 108 Ways to Be At Peace
  When Things Are Out of Control
Advanced Taekwondo
Bangkok and the Nights of Drunken Stupor
Cambodian Refugees in Long Beach, California: The Definitive Study
Chi Kung For Beginners
China Deep
Essence: The Zen of Everything
Hapkido: Essays on Self-Defense
Hapkido: The Korean Art of Self Defense
Independent Filmmaking: Secrets of the Craft
Junk: The Backstreets of Bangkok
Last Will and Testament According to the Divine Rite of the Drug Cocaine
L.A.: Tales from
  the Suburban Side of Hell
Marguerite Duras and Charles Bukowski:
  The Yin and Yang of Modern
  Erotic Literature
Mastering Health: The A to Z of Chi Kung
Nirvana in a Nutshell

No Kisses for the Sinner
On the Hard Edge of Hollywood
Sake' in a Glass, Sushi with Your Fingers:
  Fifteen Minutes in Tokyo
Samurai Zen
Shanghai Whispers Shanghai Screams
Shattered Thoughts
Suicide Slowly
Taekwondo Basics
The Ki Process:
  Korean Secrets for Cultivating Dynamic Energy
The Little Book of Yoga Breathing
The Little Book of Zen Mediation
The Most Beautiful Woman in Shanghai
The Passionate Kiss of Illusion
The Screenplays
The Tao of Self Defense
The Warrior is Silent:
  Martial Arts and the Spiritual Path
TKO: A Lost Night in Tokyo
Yoga: The Spiritual Aspects
Zen Buddhism: The Pathway to Nirvana
Zen Filmmaking
Zen in the Blink of an Eye
Zen O'clock: Time to Be
Zen: Tales from the Journey

www.ingramcontent.com/pod-product-compliance
Lightning Source LLC
Chambersburg PA
CBHW060421090426
42734CB00011B/2399